Just the Facts
Allergies

Steve Parker

Heinemann Library
Chicago, Illinois

© 2004 Heinemann Library
a division of Reed Elsevier Inc.
Chicago, Illinois

Customer Service 888-454-2279
Visit our website at www.heinemannlibrary.com

Produced by Monkey Puzzle Media
Designed by Jane Hawkins
Originated by Ambassador Litho Ltd.
Consultant: Maureen Jenkins, allergy nurse consultant
Printed and bound in China by South China Printing Company

08 07 06 05 04
10 9 8 7 6 5 4 3 2 1

Library of Congress Cataloging-in-Publication Data
Parker, Steve.
  Allergies / Steve Parker.
      p. cm. -- (Just the facts)
Summary: Defines what an allergy is, various types of allergies, some prevention and treatment methods, and other
issues related to allergic conditions.
Includes bibliographical references and index.
  ISBN 1-4034-4598-2 (Library Binding-hardcover)
  1. Allergy--Juvenile literature. [1. Allergy.] I. Title. II. Series.
  RC585.P375 2003
  616.97--dc21
                                    2003010872

Acknowledgments
The author and publisher are grateful to the following for permission to reproduce copyright material: pp. 1 (John
Durham), 5 (David Scharf),10, 11 (Dr. P. Marazzi), 13 (Susumu Nishinaga), 21 (Eye of Science), 22 (John Durham), 24 (Dr.
P. Marazzi), 25 (Jim Selby), 28 (Jerrican Gaillard), 33 (BSIP Astier), 41 (CC Studio), 42 (Jerrican Gaillard), 45 (Josh Sher),
46 (Mark Thomas), 50 (James King-Holmes) Science Photo Library; pp. 4 (Rebecca Naden/PA), 16 (Bill Lai/ ImageWorks),
18 (Journal-Courier/Steve Warmowski/ImageWorks) Topham Picturepoint; p. 6 (Musée Condé) AKG London; pp. 7, 8
Wellcome Photo Library; pp. 15 (David Kamm), 35 (Bob Jones Photography), 36 (Rob Crandell/Stock Connection Inc.)
Alamy; p. 19 (Hartmut Schwarzbach) Still Pictures; p. 23 (First Light) ImageState; p. 26 (EPA) Press Association; pp. 27,
39, 43 MPM Images; pp. 30 (Philip Bailey), 49 (Walter Smith) Corbis; pp. 31 (Organic Picture Library), 38 (Phanie Agency)
Rex Features.

Cover photograph: main image (patch test): Science Photo Library/Saturn Stills; second image: Science Photo
Library/Conor Caffrey

The cover of this book shows a young person with allergies and an allergy patch test in the background. For more
information on patch tests, turn to pages 32–33.

Special thanks to Pamela G. Richards, M.Ed., for her help in the preparation of this book.

The case studies in this book are based on factual information. In some case studies and elsewhere in this book,
names or other personal information may have been changed or omitted in order to protect the privacy of the
individuals concerned.

Contents

Allergies

Most people know someone who suffers from an allergy. Allergies are very, very widespread. In countries such as the United States, Canada, and the United Kingdom, about one adult in four has an allergy of some kind. Around the world, an estimated 500 million people suffer from allergies. They endure irritation, discomfort, pain, limits on daily life, and, in very severe cases, disability.

For some people an allergic reaction may last only a few minutes every once in a while. For others it affects them all the time, every day. For a few people, a serious allergy can even be a threat to life itself.

❝Don't forget the pollen [from the grass on the golf course]. I have allergies like a lot of other people . . . the stress of competing under those conditions in that environment definitely wears on your immune system.❞

(Tiger Woods [pictured right], U.S. golfing champion, speaking about his hay fever in 2002)

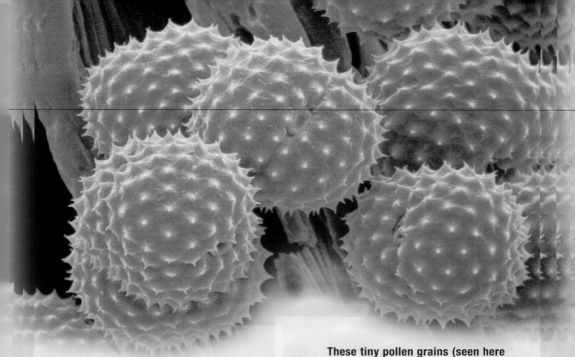

What is an allergy?

The term allergy means different things to different people. For doctors, the word allergy refers to a precise medical condition. But in daily life, the word allergy is often used in a much looser and more casual way. Coughs, colds, wheezes, skin spots, rashes, aches, pains, upset stomachs, and even hyperactive behavior are often blamed on an allergy. This is true in some cases. But in many others, the trouble is caused by germs, a small injury, stress, chemicals in food, or some other problem. The wide variation in allergic conditions, added to the variety of ways that people use the word allergy, causes much confusion about this group of health problems. This book aims to show what an allergy really is, who it affects, and how it can be treated.

These tiny pollen grains (seen here under a microscope) may look harmless, but for some people they can trigger the irritating allergy known as hay fever.

Common allergic conditions

Some of the most common conditions are listed below:

- asthma
- allergic rhinitis or hay fever
- perennial rhinitis, such as dust mite allergy
- eczema and dermatitis
- urticaria or hives
- food allergies
- allergy to venoms or poisons, such as wasp or bee stings
- allergy to drugs or medications.

History of Allergies

Today, scientists understand that an allergic reaction occurs when the body's natural defense system, called the immune system, tries to fight off a substance that is normally harmless. The immune system usually targets invading microbes—germs such as bacteria and viruses. But in a person who has an allergy, the body's defenses fight off harmless substances in the same way.

People throughout history have probably suffered from allergies. However, an allergy can often be mistaken for another health problem, such as a cough, cold, skin infection, or upset stomach. Allergies may have been occurring, without people realizing, for centuries.

Smelling flowers

One of the most common allergic reactions is to tiny particles called pollen that are released into the air by plants such as flowers, grasses, and trees. This form of allergy is generally known as hay fever or seasonal allergic rhinitis. It causes itchy and watering eyes, an itchy and runny nose, an irritated throat, sneezing, and coughing. In 1565 an Italian doctor, Leonardo Botallo, wrote one of the first medical descriptions of hay fever. Botallo described healthy people who, after smelling certain flowers, suffered a runny nose and "explosive" sneezing.

People through the ages suffered sneezing and wheezing at harvest time, but did not realize it was due to allergy.

Summer catarrh

In 1819 British physician John Bostock wrote a medical report on hay fever. He suffered from it himself. Bostock named it "summer catarrh" because it resembled a common cold, which produced catarrh (mucus and phlegm, slimy fluids produced by the body), but it happened in summer when colds were rare. In 1831 another English doctor, John Elliotson, wrote a further report on summer catarrh. One of his patients suggested that it seemed to be due to "an emanation of [something coming from] grass." This was the first mention of a substance from outside the body being the cause. Elliotson followed up the idea and people began to look for other substances that caused similar problems.

The first allergy tests

In 1880 British physician and researcher Charles Blackley wrote one of the first thorough medical books on allergy: *Hay Fever—Its Causes, Treatment, and Effective Prevention*. He carried out tests by putting a watery mixture of pollen grains into the eyes of sufferers. Not surprisingly, their eyes became very red, itchy, and swollen. At Harvard University, Morrill Wyman performed similar tests. But exactly why the body reacted in this way was still unknown.

John Elliotson (1791–1868) of University College, London, worked on a wide range of subjects, from allergies to hypnotism.

Allergy breakthroughs

About a century ago, scientists began to understand how the body of someone with an allergy reacts. In 1907 an Austrian doctor, Clemens von Pirquet, was researching the serious disease of tuberculosis (TB), when he devised the tuberculin skin test. This involved injecting tuberculin, a substance obtained from the tuberculosis germ, into the skin. If the skin reacted with a red patch or inflammation, it showed that the person had

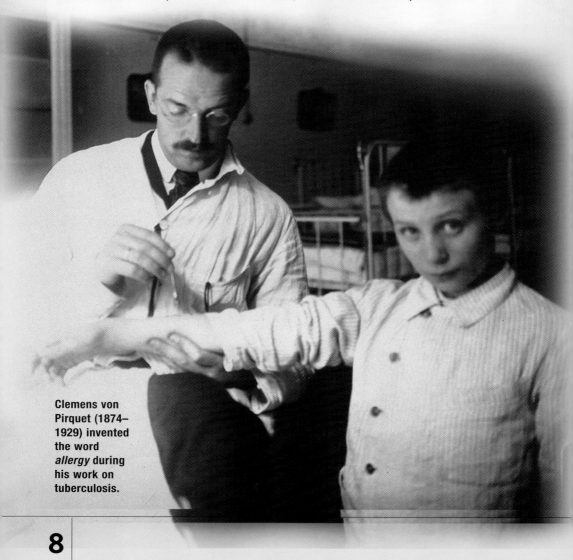

Clemens von Pirquet (1874–1929) invented the word *allergy* during his work on tuberculosis.

some resistance to the disease. Pirquet also noticed that some people reacted differently to this skin test. He invented a new term for this reaction—allergy, from two ancient Greek words, *allos* meaning "changed" or "different," and *ergos* meaning "action" or "working."

The tuberculin skin test was adapted to test people for allergies. Injecting substances extracted (obtained) from pollen into the skin caused a red, swollen, itchy lump—but only in hay fever sufferers. These people were found to be sensitive or allergic to pollen. Physician Leonard Noon began standard medical tests for sensitivity to pollen in 1911, at St Mary's Hospital, London. Similar types of tests are still used today.

Histamine

In 1904 British scientist Henry Dale began studying the substance ergot. This was obtained from a mold that grows on rye, a cereal crop. If people ate foods made from moldy rye, they suffered various effects due to the ergot, such as spasm or contraction of muscles, paralysis, sudden changes in blood pressure, and collapse.

Dale wanted to find out if ergot contained chemicals that, in pure form, might be used as helpful medical drugs. In 1910 he purified one chemical, which today is called histamine. Dale noticed that if histamine was injected into volunteers, it caused symptoms similar to those of allergies such as asthma and hay fever.

Many other scientists became interested in histamine. In 1932 medical scientists Wilhelm Feldberg (in Berlin, Germany) and Carl Dragstedt (in Chicago) discovered that histamine did not come from outside the body. They found that histamine was produced naturally by the body in the form of tiny granules inside certain microscopic cells. When these cells released their histamine in response to a trigger such as pollen, the allergic reaction occurred. In the late 1940s, research into antihistamine drugs to prevent histamine release began. By the 1950s these drugs were available, but many caused sleepiness or drowsiness. From the 1970s, improved antihistamines appeared, which caused little or no drowsiness in most sufferers.

What Is an Allergy?

Allergies produce many different symptoms, from red eyes or itchy skin, to coughing and wheezing, violent sickness, or sudden collapse. However, these are all caused by the same basic process, the allergic reaction. The differences between symptoms depend on where in the body the allergic reaction happens and how severe it is.

The main type of microscopic body cells involved in allergies are mast cells, which contain histamine, shown here as green specks.

The allergic reaction

An allergic reaction is carried out by the body's immune system. Normally, the immune system protects the body against germs and other harmful substances. But in the case of a person with an allergy, the immune system fights against a substance that is normally harmless. The substance that causes or triggers the allergic reaction is known as the allergen.

Allergens cause the immune system to react by making substances to fight them. These are called antibodies.

In the body, the antibodies stick to the allergens to damage them, as though they were germs. The antibodies also coat the surfaces of some other cells in the body, known as mast cells. These are spread throughout most of the body, but they are especially numerous near blood vessels, in the skin, and in the linings of the airways, lungs, stomach, and intestines. When allergens stick to mast cells, the cells burst open and release a chemical called histamine. Each mast cell releases about 1,000 tiny particles of histamine.

Histamine causes increased blood flow to the area and attracts various germ-fighting cells and fluids. This is part of the body's normal reaction against disease or injury. The effects are seen as inflammation—redness, soreness, and swelling due to fluid buildup. However, in an allergy there is no danger from germs.

In hay fever the allergic reaction affects the delicate surface of the eye (the conjunctiva), making it red, itchy, and watery.

The production of antibodies against allergens, the release of histamine from mast cells, and the inflammation and other effects of histamine are all known as the allergic reaction.

Sensitization

For various reasons, some people are more likely than others to develop an allergy. But the allergic reaction does not happen the first time a person encounters the allergen. After this first exposure, the person's immune system learns to recognize the allergen. This can take several days or weeks and is known as sensitization. After the period of sensitization, the allergic reaction happens each time the sufferer comes into contact with the allergen.

Types of allergen

Allergies are caused by exposure to allergens, and there are thousands of possible allergens. Some people are allergic to just one or two, while others are allergic to many different kinds. The list includes natural substances such as plant pollen; tiny flakes of animal skin, fur, or bird feathers (called dander); tiny spores from molds and fungi; and powdery droppings from minute creatures called dust mites. Many modern artificial products and chemicals can cause allergies or allergy-like reactions. These are found in dyes, clothes, cosmetics, foods, food additives, industrial cleaners, soaps and detergents, certain medical drugs, and metal products. The list grows longer every year.

Targeting different areas

Allergens come into contact with the body in many different ways. Some touch an outer part such as the skin or eyes or are breathed into the nose, throat, and lungs. Others may be eaten and reach the stomach and digestive system, or they may be injected into the body in the form of medication. The way that the allergen makes contact with the body affects the symptoms. For example, in hay fever (seasonal rhinitis), floating pollen grains in the air land on the sensitive covering of the eye and are breathed into the moist inner linings of the nose and throat. These, therefore, are the areas that suffer the main allergic reaction.

Allergic reactions tend to happen in mucus membranes. These are thin, moist, delicate layers that form the outer coverings or inner linings of many body parts—the nose, throat, airways, lungs, stomach, and intestines.

A frightening meal

Neil Drummond, eighteen, lives in London. Neil first discovered that he had a food allergy when he was eight, on a family vacation to the south of France. One evening in a restaurant he ordered *bouillabaisse*, a type of seafood stew. Neil took just a few sips of *bouillabaisse* and decided he did not like it. Within a few minutes, he had itchy red blotches on his skin, and his neck and chin were swollen. He soon felt better, but his parents suspected he might be allergic to seafood, so they avoided it for the rest of the vacation. Back at home, Neil went to the doctor and tests showed he was allergic to shellfish.

This is a magnified photo of the
lining of the inside of the nose.
The hairlike cilia, designed to
trap tiny bits of dust and germs,
also trap pollen grains, which
cause hay fever.

A Deadly Reaction

Anaphylaxis

Sometimes, in rare cases, an allergic reaction can be life threatening. It starts at the site affected by the allergen, but it gathers speed and severity and spreads through the body in minutes, causing skin rash, redness, itching, and swelling. This condition is known as anaphylaxis (from the Greek words *ana* and *phulaxis*, meaning "overprotection"). Accumulation of fluid is noticeable around the face, hands, and feet, which look puffy. Fluid also gathers in the airways and lungs, which may become tighter, affecting a person's breathing. Victims may feel weak with a headache, stomach pains, heart flutters, and a sense of panic. They may faint or collapse as the body's blood pressure falls. If they are not treated in time, they may even die.

Who is at risk?

In countries such as the United States and the United Kingdom, anaphylaxis is the reason for about one in every 500 visits to an emergency room. It is difficult to predict if an allergic reaction will develop into anaphylaxis.

However, if a person has suffered from anaphylaxis before, then it is more likely to occur when exposure to the same allergen happens again.

Almost any type of allergy can lead to anaphylaxis. However, most cases involve food allergies, especially to nuts such as peanuts, Brazil nuts, walnuts, and almonds (this includes some nut oils as well). Other food culprits are shellfish such as prawns and oysters, fish, sesame seeds, eggs, milk, and dairy products. Anaphylaxis may also occur with allergies to wasp or bee venom or to drugs such as antibiotics.

Every second counts

Anaphylaxis is a medical emergency. Seconds count. The vital treatment is an injection of a substance called adrenaline, which reverses the life-threatening effects in the body, in addition to other drugs. Even if a person recovers from apparent anaphylaxis without treatment, he or she should see a doctor for a medical checkup.

Emergency!

Someone suffering from anaphylaxis needs first aid from an expert, who will follow the procedure below:

1. HELP They will summon emergency help such as an ambulance or paramedic by the quickest means, usually telephone.

2. BREATHING The first-aid expert will put the person in whatever position breathing is easiest, usually lying with legs raised.

3. INFORMATION The expert can ask a conscious victim if he or she has had anaphylaxis before and what should be done.

4. MEDICATION The expert will check the patient for medication. Some at-risk people carry their own medication, such as pills or a ready-loaded pen-type injection syringe, or they have a card, bracelet, necklace, or other item with an emergency phone number to call.

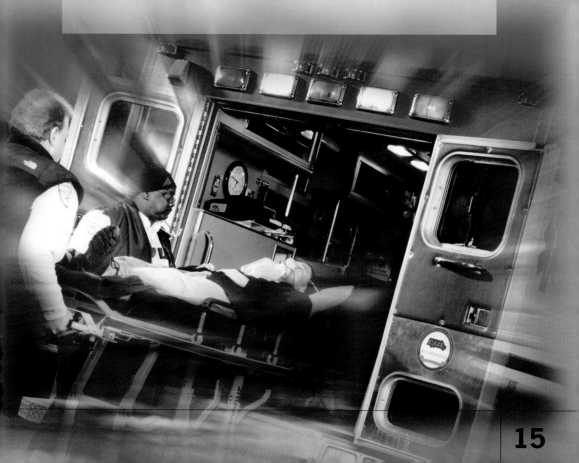

Who Is Affected?

The reasons why only some people develop allergies are not well understood. It is not possible to predict if or when a person will develop an allergy. However, various factors make certain groups of people more likely to develop them.

Family history

Allergies are believed to run in families. Several people in a family may have the same allergy, such as hay fever, or they may have different allergies. This suggests that they have inherited

genes from their parents that made them more likely than other people to develop an allergy. This is called an inherited susceptibility or predisposition to allergy. However, the numbers of genes and exactly what they do are not yet understood. Also, having these genes does not mean that a person will definitely develop an allergy. In general, the chances of developing an allergy are higher for:

- a person whose close family members suffer from allergies;
- a boy rather than a girl;
- a person from a small family of one or two children, rather than a larger family;
- a person whose mother smoked or did not eat healthily during pregnancy.

Early life

Home surroundings during the first months and years of life can affect a person's chances of developing an allergy. However, the reasons why are not well understood. The chances can

Babies who are bottle-fed rather than breast-fed may be slightly more likely to develop an allergy. But the chances are very small.

be higher for a child who grows up in a house where people smoke or for a baby who is fed from a bottle (with formula) rather than breast-fed. Changing from liquid to solid foods relatively early makes it slightly more likely for a child to develop an allergy, as does living in an area with polluted air, or going to a nursery or day care center from a young age. But even if all of these conditions apply to a certain person, this still does not mean that he or she will definitely develop an allergy. It simply increases the likelihood.

Allergies and age

More young children have allergies than older children and adults. In some countries such as the United States and the United Kingdom, almost half of babies and children with allergies such as eczema or hay fever have grown out of them by the age of 25. Also, the later in life an allergy develops, the more likely it is to last for many years, rather than fade away after a few years. But it is difficult to predict any individual case.

A growing problem

Allergies are becoming more common. In the past twenty years in industrialized countries such as the United States, the numbers of allergy sufferers have increased by three or even four times. It is estimated that one person in three under the age of eighteen has some form of allergy.

Some aspects of early life can decrease the risk of developing an allergy. For example, a child who grows up in a house with pets such as cats and dogs or on a farm may be less likely to develop an allergic condition. Another statistic shows that children who have suffered certain diseases caused by viruses, such as measles, may have less chance of developing an allergy afterward. (Of course, these statistics do not take into account the risks of infection from these viruses, which could be more harmful than a mild allergy.)

In general, children from rural areas are slightly less likely to develop an allergy.

Children in city areas with polluted air have a slightly greater chance of developing an allergy.

Hygiene hypothesis

One theory for the increasing number of allergies is called the hygiene hypothesis. Broadly, it says that children who are brought up in very clean, hygienic, germ-free surroundings become more at risk of developing allergies. This is because their bodies do not regularly encounter germs and natural allergens in small amounts over the months and years. This means they have less general resistance to fight off health problems.

Linked to the hygiene hypothesis is the idea that people in more developed and industrialized regions are more likely to have allergies than people in more rural areas and less developed countries. One reason might be that people in industrialized regions are more likely to come into contact with a wide range of artificial substances, including food additives, industrial chemicals, pollutants in the air, and mass-produced products, which could act as allergens.

Richer industrialized countries usually have established healthcare systems, with many doctors and hospitals, and more time and money to test people for allergies and record the results. In contrast, people from poorer regions face much greater problems, such as eating enough food to stay alive. In the face of such difficulties, allergies become minor matters that are perhaps not recorded.

Allergies in the Nose

Some allergic conditions affect mainly the nose and cause symptoms similar to those of a common cold. Indeed, some people seem to have a common cold all the time. They sniff with a stuffed up or runny nose, blow their nose often, and cough to clear their throat. They often get headaches, sore throats, and earaches. Their eyes may be red and runny. Their stuffed up nose may cause snoring and disturbed sleep.

Perennial allergic rhinitis

These are all symptoms of an allergy called perennial (or persistent) allergic rhinitis. Rhinitis is when the nose is affected by inflammation—swelling, redness, soreness, and fluid buildup. It occurs mainly in the delicate linings of the air spaces inside the nose, which produce excess mucus. It is called perennial rhinitis because it tends to occur all through the year, unlike seasonal rhinitis or hay fever.

It is estimated that between one in eight and one in four people suffer from perennial allergic rhinitis. It tends to begin in childhood and is usually caused by an allergy to tiny floating particles that are breathed in from the air. One of the main allergens is the microscopic droppings of the dust mite. This tiny creature is smaller than the dot on this *i* and lives among bits of dust, flakes of skin, and other debris, in almost any nook or cranny, especially indoors. Its droppings dry out, turn to powder, and float in the air. Other allergens for perennial rhinitis are dander (microflakes of skin, fur, or feathers from almost any kind of pet or other animal), plant pollen, or microspores from molds and fungi.

People with perennial allergic rhinitis often notice that their symptoms are worse indoors and in places where the allergens collect, such as rooms that are dusty or often used by pets. Some people encounter the allergens regularly due to their work or hobbies, especially if they regularly come into contact with old hay or straw, mushrooms or fungi, or old or moldy bird droppings.

The droppings of the dust mite are one of the main allergens that trigger perennial allergic rhinitis.

"Sometimes I just want to cut my nose off and put it in a bowl of cold water to wash it out and stop it from itching."

(Anna, a fifteen-year-old allergic rhinitis sufferer)

Hay fever and similar allergies

Perennial allergic rhinitis tends to occur all year. Seasonal allergic rhinitis, as the name suggests, is usually worse at a certain time of year, generally spring or summer, when trees, grass, and weeds produce their flowers. These release tiny grains of pollen that float to other flowers of the same kind, so that seeds can be produced. However, some of the pollen floats into people's noses and throats and lands on their eyes. In some people this causes an allergic reaction.

Seasonal allergic rhinitis is often called hay fever. But it is not only triggered by pollen from hay. Almost any pollen from flowers, herbs, grasses, bushes, or trees can be the cause.

Some people are affected by several types of pollen over a long period, three months or more. Others are allergic to only one or two types and suffer for just a few days while that particular plant is in bloom.

The fever part of the name comes from the similarity of the symptoms to those of a fever or raised temperature, making the sufferer feel sick. They include a runny nose, with sneezing and sniffing and itching; red, sore, runny, and itchy eyes; a sore or irritated throat; coughing; and irritated palate (roof of the mouth) and ears. Symptoms may worsen in episodes or attacks, which last about 15–30 minutes, then disappear for a while.

In the United States, an estimated 36 million people—roughly one in eight—suffer from seasonal allergic rhinitis. About 1 person in 30 consults a doctor each year because of it. According to the American College of Allergy, Asthma, and Immunology, allergies are the sixth leading cause of chronic disease in the United States.

❝Sometimes I don't know whether to sing into the mike, or cough or sneeze all over it.❞

(Nina Persson, vocalist and songwriter with the award-winning band The Cardigans. She suffers from hay fever.)

Skin Allergies

Skin spots, lumps, sores, and rashes are very common symptoms of allergies. However, some of these problems are not allergy-based, but are caused by chemicals such as household cleaners or strong detergents that irritate and damage the skin. These substances affect everyone, allergic or not. In countries such as the United States and the United Kingdom, allergy-based skin conditions occur in about one child in seven, and one adult in ten, at some time in their lives.

Urticaria

Urticaria is also called hives. It appears as raised lumps or pale, flat-topped patches called welts, with reddish skin around. The welts are itchy, and they may come and go on different parts of the body. Urticaria usually disappears in a few hours. However, it may occur as part of a serious medical condition called anaphylaxis.

Eczema and dermatitis

This group of skin conditions has many causes and different names. In general, the skin becomes red, inflamed, itchy, and sore. Almost any part of the body is vulnerable, although the face, arms, and legs are often affected, and particularly the skin creases at joints like the elbow and knee. In babies and children the problem is usually called atopic or infantile eczema. The skin may become scabby. In adults the skin is drier and more scaly, and the problem is more likely to be called a skin contact allergy or dermatitis.

Urticaria is sometimes known as nettle rash because the poisons in stinging nettles produce a similar effect on the skin.

This girl has eczema. She is using a cream prescribed by her doctor.

Causes

The causes of allergic skin conditions vary greatly. It is estimated that food allergy is involved in more than a quarter of eczema-affected babies and children. Animal-based allergens that float in the air and touch the skin, such as dust mite droppings and animal dander are also causes. Heat, cold, humidity, or bright sunlight can also trigger a skin allergy. Other causes include stress or excitement, exercise that causes sweating, or some types of fabric, such as wool or nylon.

Chemical allergens

A growing range of products and chemicals can provoke allergic skin conditions. These chemical allergens are found in:

- cosmetics, soaps, perfumes, shampoos, shower gels, hair dyes;
- laundry detergents and fabric conditioners (often biological or enzyme types);
- disinfectants and chemical cleaners;
- rubber and latex materials;
- leather (especially if treated and dyed);
- glues and solvents;
- mechanical lubricants such as oils and greases;
- construction materials such as cements, fillers, and sealants;
- pure metals, such as nickel (found in some bracelets), belt buckles, buttons, zippers, earrings, piercing studs, and other items that come into contact with skin.

Food Allergies

About 20 adults out of 100 say they have suffered from a food allergy. However, if these twenty people underwent medical tests, true allergies would be discovered in only one or two of them. This is partly explained by other reactions to foods—intolerance, toxicity, and aversion. Food intolerance is not a true allergy, but it does trigger processes in the body that result in allergy-like symptoms. They may be due to a lack of a digestive chemical in an individual, or the food may contain the chemical histamine.

In food toxicity, the food contains harmful or poisonous substances that would affect anyone, whether they have an allergy or not. People with food aversion are genuinely convinced that they are allergic to a certain food, but medical tests show no allergic reaction.

Symptoms

Symptoms of a genuine food allergy include a widespread skin rash that may itch, as well as swelling of body parts (noticeable on the face, feet, and hands), and problems with breathing, such as wheezing. Longer-term effects may include eczema, headaches, and behavior changes such as hyperactivity. Some cases involve abdominal pain, vomiting, diarrhea, and irregular heartbeats (palpitations), but these also occur in food intolerance rather than true allergy. In oral allergy syndrome, the mouth and throat become red and itchy.

"I was lethargic, very tired, with a rash on my forearms so itchy it drove me crazy. . . ."

(Amanda Donohoe [pictured left], British actress, talking about her wheat allergy in 2001)

In rare but an increasing number of cases, food allergy can threaten a person's life (see pages 40–41).

The main culprits

Almost any food can provoke a reaction. However, six main food ingredients cause nine-tenths of allergy cases in younger people: cow's milk, egg white (albumen), wheat, white fish, peanuts, and soybeans. These foods occur widely, but sometimes they are hidden. Milk and eggs, for example, are basic cooking ingredients, many breads are baked with wheat (in the form of flour), and soy is found in a wide range of processed and prepared foods.

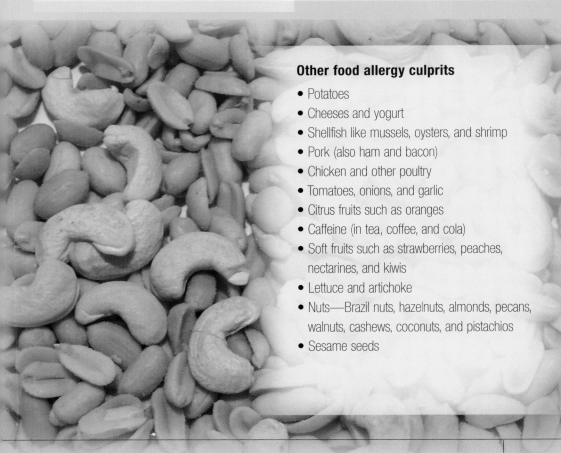

Other food allergy culprits

- Potatoes
- Cheeses and yogurt
- Shellfish like mussels, oysters, and shrimp
- Pork (also ham and bacon)
- Chicken and other poultry
- Tomatoes, onions, and garlic
- Citrus fruits such as oranges
- Caffeine (in tea, coffee, and cola)
- Soft fruits such as strawberries, peaches, nectarines, and kiwis
- Lettuce and artichoke
- Nuts—Brazil nuts, hazelnuts, almonds, pecans, walnuts, cashews, coconuts, and pistachios
- Sesame seeds

Drugs and Microbes

About one person in twenty has an allergic reaction to a particular drug or medication. This may be in the form of pills, tablets, liquid, droplets, injection, lotion, cream, or ointment. The number of people reporting such reactions is about one in eight, but most of these cases are not allergies. They are due to the illness itself, or to taking too much medicine, or to the medicine's side effects.

Drugs can be allergens

The symptoms of a drug allergy usually appear within one or two hours and often involve an itchy rash like eczema or urticaria. More rarely there are longer-term effects several days later, with further skin rashes and problems with internal organs such as the liver and kidneys. In rare cases there is a sudden, serious reaction called anaphylaxis.

Almost any kind of drug or medication might cause an allergy, although most cases are rare. Examples include antibiotic drugs such as penicillin, anesthetics, muscle-relaxing drugs used before operations or for painful muscle spasms, various heart drugs, and common painkillers such as aspirin and ibuprofen. Some people even become allergic to the antiseptic soaps and lotions used to clean wounds and kill germs. Others may be allergic to immunizations (vaccines), such as those given to babies and children against diseases such as diphtheria and tetanus.

Whenever a drug is prescribed, medical guidelines urge doctors and pharmacists to check with patients about allergies. People with allergies to medication should mention this to doctors and pharmacists. In some cases patients should wear a Medic Alert bracelet.

Allergy to infection

People can develop allergies to various microbes or germs, such as bacteria and viruses, that cause infectious diseases. The first time the microbes enter the body, they multiply and cause their particular illness in the usual way. But after this first exposure, some people become allergic or sensitized to that particular germ. When they encounter that germ again, they suffer an allergic reaction, with symptoms similar to those described above for a drug allergy. Examples of infections that people may become allergic to include glandular fever and hepatitis B.

Bites and Stings

A sting from a bee or wasp can be painful and distressing. Some people develop allergies to the poisons or venoms in these stings. They suffer much more pain than a person who does not have an allergy, with redness and swelling and sometimes a skin rash such as urticaria. All of these symptoms last longer than from a normal sting. Other animals' bites or stings can also provoke an allergic reaction. These include ants, gnats, mosquitoes, snakes, scorpions, jellyfish, and even the stinging hairs on woolly-bear caterpillars.

Symptoms of the allergic reaction increase the body's normal reaction to the venom. They are usually concentrated at the site of the sting and develop quickly over minutes. If the bite is on the ankle, for example, then the pain, swelling, and redness

may spread into the foot and up the leg to the knee. The affected body part becomes stiff, tense, and achy, and movements are painful. There may be severe itching and more widespread swelling, light-headedness, and other serious symptoms that can rapidly develop into a life threatening condition called anaphylaxis.

Mild to serious stings

Wasp and hornet stings are usually the most serious. Wasps can use their stingers several times, causing more harm than a bee, which can use its stinger only once. Effects on the body depend on the sting site and the degree of allergy in the person, and can vary from mild to life-threatening. Experts estimate that from 40 to 100 people die each year in the United States from serious allergic reaction to stinging insects.

A scare for Alan

Alan is twelve and lives in Peekskill, New York. When Alan was eight, he was enjoying a family summer picnic when he was stung on the wrist—by what, no one saw. Alan cried in shock and pain. The swelling and redness quickly spread up his arm. His parents took him to the nearest medical center. Alan was having an allergic reaction to the sting. The allergic reaction was treated and gradually faded. Alan and his parents received valuable advice about avoiding such problems in the future and about first aid in case of anaphylaxis.

Diagnosis and Support

Is it an allergy?

Most people who think they may have an allergy should visit their doctor. The doctor asks various questions about the symptoms—when they occur, for how long, and what appears to cause them—in order to determine what the allergen could be. It helps if the person has kept notes about when allergic reactions occur. Some people keep a food diary, recording everything they eat, or a place diary of rooms and other sites visited, noting any allergic reactions they may have. Follow-up medical tests, either at a health center or at an allergy clinic, may identify the allergen more precisely.

Skin prick test

Skin prick tests involve putting several droplets of fluid, each containing an allergen, in rows on the skin, usually on the forearm. The skin under each droplet is pricked with a small needle so that the

allergen can enter the body. An allergic reaction is marked by a small, swollen, pale, raised, and itchy area at the prick site. It develops within fifteen to twenty minutes then gradually fades. The bigger the affected area, the greater the reaction.

Patch and blood tests

In the patch test, small discs coated with potential allergens are taped to the skin, usually for 48 hours. The skin areas are studied for reactions such as eczema or dermatitis. Blood samples may also be taken and

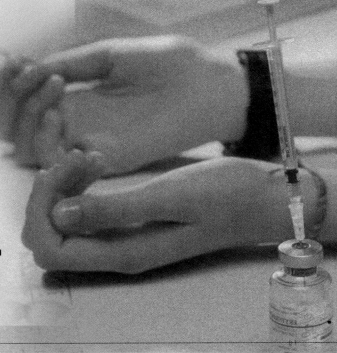

Patch tests on the skin can even reveal reactions to allergens that normally cause symptoms elsewhere, such as in the nose.

analyzed in the laboratory. If a person has reacted to the allergens before, there will be antibodies against them in the blood.

Challenge tests

In a challenge test, the person is directly exposed to a suspected allergen under strict medical conditions. In the case of food allergy, the person may not be told that the suspected food is in a meal or pill. This helps to screen out nonallergic reactions such as food aversion.

Maureen's allergy

Maureen lives in Brisbane, Australia. When she was fourteen, she suffered stomach pains after some meals. Maureen's older brother, Jim, had severe asthma, and her parents knew that allergies run in families. They thought Maureen might have a food allergy. Over several weeks Maureen kept a food diary of exactly what she ate. The stomach pains varied but there was no clear link with a particular food. Finally Maureen went to her family doctor. After a few tests the problem was identified as a stomach ulcer. Maureen discovered that stomach pain, on its own, is rarely a symptom of food allergy.

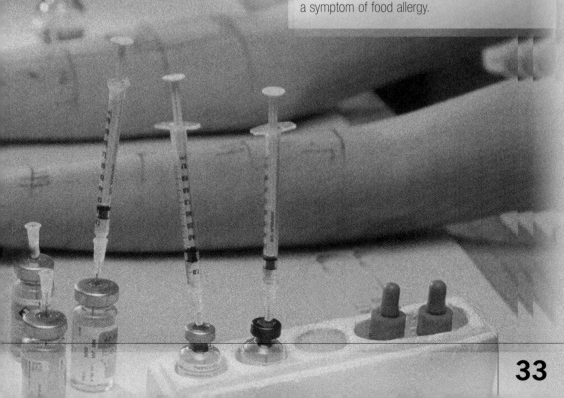

Tackling an allergy

For many health problems—such as a common cold or sprained wrist—people usually suffer for a while, then get better. However, an allergy may have far-reaching and long-lasting effects on everyday life. Medical treatments can lessen the symptoms and allow the patient greater freedom. But people with allergies can also help themselves. They can keep their allergy under control by taking responsibility for their condition and having a positive attitude, rather than trying to ignore symptoms.

People who can help

Many professionals in the healthcare system can offer advice about coping with an allergy. They include the family doctor, health center professionals, and allergy specialists, who are usually based at allergy clinics. Dietitians can offer valuable advice for food allergies and dermatologists are specially trained to treat skin allergies. There is also a huge range of complementary practitioners. In addition, there are many self-help groups run by people with allergies. They share their experiences and knowledge and pass on useful advice and practical tips to other people with allergies. Teachers and school counselors can also offer advice and support to allergy sufferers.

Support from family and friends

Family and friends of a person with an allergy play an important role. Their understanding, tolerance, and patience can help the person to cope well, rather than feeling like a burden on others. People with allergies may at times feel picked on or singled out because of their condition. They may not want to go outside on a sunny summer day, for example, because they know in a few minutes they will be sneezing with itchy eyes from hay fever. But their friends and family might misinterpret this as being cowardly or not interested in exercise or sports. People with allergies sometimes become angry or depressed. Younger children with an allergy may not understand their condition. They often feel annoyed or left out because they cannot eat certain foods, or have pets, or play outside like their friends do.

Family and friends can give support and encouragement at these times. At the same time, they can watch for signs that the sufferer is becoming obsessed or dominated by the allergy and letting it affect daily life unduly.

"Why me?" is a common question for people with long-term health problems. But dwelling on the negative side can make things feel worse.

Living with Allergies

Coping with an allergy in daily life can be a balancing act. On one side is
the need to be aware of the problem, take precautions, and avoid the
allergen as much as possible. This reduces symptoms, suffering,
the need for medication, and the possible risk of serious
allergic reaction. On the other side is the problem of
taking so much care and so many
precautions that everyday life
becomes unreasonably

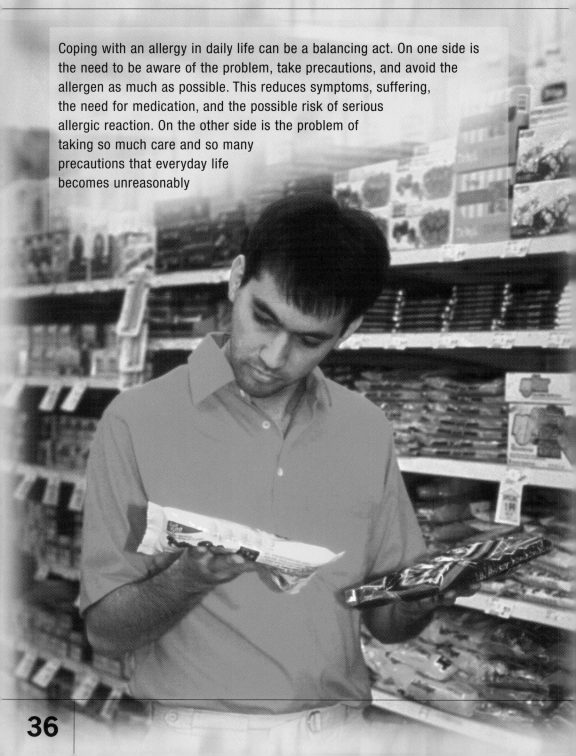

restricted, with constant worry and fear of being exposed to the allergen.

Many people with allergies develop the habit of adding the word *allergy* to any lists, plans, or arrangements they make. A day in the country, eating at a friend's house, a vacation, or a shopping trip for foods or household goods could all lead to allergen exposure. It is important to anticipate if exposure is likely and to take precautions such as having antihistamine medication available.

Allergies at home

People spend a lot of time at home, and this is where they have greatest control over their surroundings. For many types of allergies, practical precautions can be carried out at home to avoid exposure to allergens. Perennial rhinitis, for example, is caused by an allergy to dust mite droppings. Therefore, it is important to take extra care when cleaning and to remove dust from nooks and crannies. A vacuum cleaner with an allergen filter is more effective than an ordinary vacuum cleaner. Dust-proof covers on mattresses, comforters, pillows, and cushions also reduce the risk. Air and dust filters can also be useful.

For someone with a food allergy, it is important to check all food items for the allergenic food or ingredient. When buying foods, all food packages and labels should be checked to make sure the allergen is not contained in any of the products. Labeling regulations are gradually improving in this respect. In most countries, for example, food packaging must clearly state if a food may contain nuts or even traces of nuts.

There are similar practical tips for other allergies. Family members and friends can help by understanding the problems of the person with the allergy, suggesting ideas, and keeping a lookout for times when exposure to the allergen may occur.

People with food allergies should check labels to make sure that possible allergens are not contained in the foods they buy.

Let the person control the allergy—not the other way around.

(Advice for coping with an allergy in daily life)

Away from home

For many people with allergies, there are fewer worries about being at home, compared to being out and about, where they have less control over the environment. School, college, work, or even vacation spots are all places where a person might come into contact with possible allergens.

Taking simple precautions such as remembering to pack allergy medication makes sure that a vacation is safe, comfortable, and fun!

Planning ahead

Before going out, it helps to think ahead and make plans to minimize exposure to allergens. When eating out at a restaurant, for example, it is advised to call ahead to discuss any food allergy with the chef. With enough warning, the staff can offer alternative dishes. This avoids the problem of turning up for the meal to find that choosing a dish is difficult, which may spoil an otherwise pleasant experience.

For any allergy, planning ahead helps to avoid situations in which the sufferer is put in an awkward position, requiring special treatment. This draws unwanted attention to the allergy. The person with the allergy may feel guilty or at fault. For most types of allergies, there are lists of protective measures, precautions, and useful equipment that can reduce allergen exposure. This applies especially to places where people spend a lot of time, such as classrooms or workplaces. Schools, colleges, and employers usually have legal duties to take into account more serious allergies, although the regulations differ from region to region. A child who suffers severe hay fever, for example, can avoid exposure to pollen by being allowed to stay indoors at school during the main hay fever season. A person with a food allergy can have this taken into account when meals are prepared at school or work—just like for people with other dietary requirements, such as those with diabetes.

Kelly's plate of food

Kelly is eight years old and lives in Toronto, Canada. Kelly is allergic to wheat. When she was younger, Kelly's allergy caused problems for her at school. The staff always tried to disguise the fact that her meals were specially prepared, and they could not understand why Kelly got upset. It turned out that it was not the food that caused the problem, but the plate. To identify her meal, the staff used a different color of plate for Kelly, but she did not like being seen as different than her friends.

Kirsty's story

On Kirsty's tenth birthday, she went bowling with some girlfriends. The girls were having a great time. After the first game they took a break for snacks and drinks. Kirsty was very excited, with the bowling and her birthday. She forgot to do what she had been doing for years—to check that her food contained no nuts or nut traces of any kind.

When Kirsty was two, just after eating peanut butter on toast, she became very ill and could not breathe properly. Her parents rushed her to the hospital. Soon afterward, tests showed that Kirsty had an allergy to some nuts. Since then, Kirsty's parents always avoided giving her any nuts, even tiny traces such as nut oils or flavorings. Sometimes it meant having special meals, but they all got used to it. Kirsty often checked her own snacks and meals, read food labels, and asked if there were any nuts in any food she was given. But, on her birthday, she forgot. After eating an ice cream she felt lightheaded and breathless and collapsed in a chair. A bowling center employee called an ambulance. In the ambulance, Kirsty was given an adrenaline injection (adrenaline increases heart rate and blood pressure and helps open up the airways, making it easier to breathe).

At the hospital, Kirsty recovered quickly.

Medical specialists called allergists can provide useful advice to prevent an allergy from interfering with daily life.

A few days later, Kirsty visited her own doctor with her parents for a checkup. The doctor arranged for new tests. The tests showed exactly what she was allergic to, and how strongly. The doctor also arranged for her to see an allergy specialist the following week. Kirsty said the specialist was "brilliant." She told Kirsty about the many kinds of medicines to help an allergy, and how new ones were always on the market. She advised Kirsty to wear a special bracelet or necklace to warn others about her allergy, and to carry a card with information about what to do in an emergency. Best of all, the allergist gave Kirsty many useful tips about how to check foods and meals for nuts, and how to remember to do this every day—even on birthdays!

Prevention and Treatment

Treating symptoms

There is a wide range of products and preparations available that can reduce the symptoms of an allergic reaction and ease suffering. They include eye drops, skin creams, and nasal sprays.

Pharmacists, doctors, allergy specialists, or self-help groups can provide useful advice.

Substances called emollients are particularly useful for allergies that affect the skin, such as forms of eczema or dermatitis. These conditions can be distressing for babies and young children, who do not understand what is happening and why they should not scratch such an annoying itch. Emollients soften, moisturize, and soothe the skin. They come in the form of creams, ointments, oils, and lotions, and can be spread on the skin or added to bath water.

Allergy eye drops can help soothe red, itchy eyes and also wash away the allergen.

Additional advice for preventing and treating eczema or dermatitis includes:

- Avoid soaps, gels, and shampoos. Even some hypoallergenic types (which contain very low amounts of possible allergens) can cause problems. People with eczema or dermatitis should try different types of hypoallergenic products to find out which ones work best.
- Pat rather than rub the skin dry.
- Wear loose-fitting clothes with cotton next to the skin.
- As much as possible, avoid strong emotions, worry, and stress. These can worsen many allergic conditions, especially eczema or dermatitis.

Food additives

Numerous substances added to foods can cause allergic reactions or food intolerance. These substances are more common in processed, prepared, packaged, and take-out foods. In the United States these additives are regulated by the Food and Drug Administration (FDA). In 1985, the FDA set up the Adverse Reaction Monitoring System (ARMS), which monitors the effects of additives in food, cosmetics, and drugs.

Brightly colored sweets usually contain food dyes or colorings.

Food additives that cause complaints

The Adverse Reaction Monitoring System (ARMS) receives numerous complaints regarding reactions to food additives. The most common complaints include:

- Aspartame. This artificial sweetener is used to replace sugar in many products. It accounts for over 75 percent of complaints to ARMS regarding food additives.
- Sulfites. An estimated one percent of people are sensitive to sulfites.
- Monosodium glutamate. This flavor enhancer must be listed on product labels, but glutamate can sometimes occur naturally in foods.
- Nitrates/nitrites. These preservatives enhance flavors and colors of meat products.

Medications

Medications used to treat allergies vary from mild, over-the-counter versions to powerful prescription drugs. Since allergies are so varied, a drug that works for one sufferer may not suit another, even for the same allergy. Anyone with an allergy should consult a healthcare professional before using a particular treatment. There are a wide range of drugs available, and a person with an allergy, with advice from a doctor or pharmacist, can test various products to find out which is most effective in his or her case.

Antihistamines

Antihistamines reduce the effect of histamine, the main body chemical that causes allergic reaction. Antihistamines decrease itching and may help other symptoms. They are especially useful for hay fever and other forms of rhinitis and for some skin conditions. There are dozens of different types available. Many come in pill, tablet, or liquid form, while some are applied directly to the affected area as ointments or drops. Certain types work very quickly but only for a short time, while all-day versions act for many hours.

Steroids

Steroid (corticosteroid) drugs prevent or reduce swelling, congestion, redness, and other features of inflammation. Preventers are taken regularly in low doses to prevent symptoms. Relievers are used

if symptoms are likely to begin. Steroids may be inhaled as a nasal spray, taken as eye drops (under medical supervision), or as pills (also under medical supervision).

Decongestants

Decongestant nasal sprays or tablets can also be helpful, especially for hay fever and other rhinitis sufferers. However, they should only be used for a short time. If used for longer periods, the congestion tends to comes back more severely.

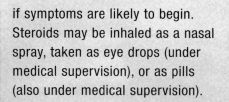

Warning

For any drug, it is important to read the information on the package and leaflet inside. Some drugs, including certain antihistamines, cause side effects such as drowsiness or sleepiness. For this reason, they are not recommended when people need to be alert, such as when driving, operating machinery, or even taking tests. Steroids, in particular, should be taken only under strict medical supervision and according to the instructions.

Complementary therapies

In the United States, it is estimated that from one quarter to one half of people with allergies who have consulted doctors in the conventional healthcare system also consult complementary or alternative practitioners at some time.

There are many reasons why people explore other treatments. Some people with allergies feel that they have low priority among busy doctors, who have stressful workloads and can only give limited time to each patient. They appreciate the greater time and attention that a complementary practitioner may be able to offer.

An acupuncturist inserts very sharp, sterile needles into the body to affect its flow of vital energy.

They may also feel they are being understood and treated as a whole person, rather than simply being offered medical drugs for specific symptoms. Some people believe that complementary treatments or alternative therapies might be safer and more natural, with fewer side effects than conventional medicines. Some explore complementary methods for the reason that the name suggests—to complement, or add to, their other treatments.

Range of complementary therapies

Some of the better-known therapies for allergies include herbal and Bach flower remedies, homeopathy, and acupuncture. In acupuncture, sharp needles are placed into the body at certain points to affect the flow of what practitioners call *chi* or vital energy through the body. For a food allergy, for example, the needle points are chosen to direct energy to the stomach and intestines so the energy is able to overcome the allergic reaction.

Certain people suffer more from their allergies when they are stressed out or worried. They find that relaxation techniques such as yoga and hypnotherapy may help. For others, a person called a clinical ecologist considers many aspects of the environment and surroundings at home and work and play, including water, air, food, housing, daily habits, and levels of pollution, to discover causes or triggers of the allergy.

Success rates

The response of individual patients to these therapies is difficult to predict. Also, scientific studies show that success rates of many therapies are often no greater than would be expected by chance. However, it is accepted that most of these techniques have helped some allergy sufferers. People who consider trying these types of treatments are advised to make contact with a practitioner through their own doctor or an established national organization.

Can Allergies Be Cured?

In the same way that an allergy can develop at almost any age, it can also fade at any time. The medical reasons for this are unclear. But doctors often reassure patients that for common allergies such as eczema and hay fever, "age is the best cure." Statistics show that many babies and children gradually lose their allergies through their teenage years or twenties. For every ten babies and toddlers who develop eczema, about five will no longer suffer from it by six years of age, and another four will be free of it ten years later. Some cures claimed by allergy treatments may simply be this natural tendency for people to lose allergies with age.

Desensitization

Desensitization is when the body is exposed to gradually increasing amounts of allergen. This is usually given by injection at regular intervals, such as weekly. The complete course lasts three years or more. The technique tends to work best for a person sensitive to only one allergen, such as a single type of plant pollen. It requires strict medical supervision due to the small risk of a severe allergic reaction after an injection. Patients visit a specialist for injections, and must wait for one hour afterward until the risk period for severe reaction has passed. Desensitization is also known as desensitization immunotherapy, allergen-specific immunotherapy (SIT), or allergy injections or shots.

Desensitization is more popular with doctors in some countries than others. It is most successful in treating breathed-in allergens, such as pollen, and also against venoms such as bee and wasp stings. However, it requires regular attendance by the patient for injections over a long period, and it can be costly. There is no guarantee of success. Surveys show that desensitization works well in many cases.

James is cured

James, age sixteen, lived in Sheffield, England, and had suffered from hay fever since he was five years old. When he was ten, his family moved to a village on the coast. At the time of the move, his parents worried that James's hay fever would worsen. In fact, it almost disappeared. The local doctor suggested that James was probably allergic to pollen from city-park trees that did not grow near his new home. Also, winds tended to blow in from the sea, and so carried less pollen of all kinds.

Some allergy sufferers find that the cleaner air of coastal regions can reduce their symptoms.

Hopes for the future

Many areas of research try to make allergies less of a problem. For example, millions of allergy sufferers use medication as the most convenient form of control. So drug companies continue to develop new antihistamines, steroids, and other drugs that work better and have fewer side effects.

The main progress in allergy research is toward more effective and safer medications. This immunologist is testing new treatments on human tissue. She is looking for inflamed cells— a sign of an allergic reaction.

Various public health measures could help allergy sufferers. These include banning smoking and reducing heating in public places such as shopping malls; providing clearer warnings of possible allergens on packaging, especially for foods and skin products; and planting more low-allergy grasses, flowers, and trees in parks, gardens, and farms. However, such measures often lose out to other demands for safeguarding the public, such as improving road safety.

Sublingual therapy

A newer form of desensitization is SLIT, sublingual immunotherapy. Increasing amounts of the allergen are given daily as drops under the tongue. This may end the need to visit allergy specialists for injections and also reduce the risk of severe allergic reaction. Early results have been encouraging, but there are still many trials and safety tests to pass before it can become a widely adopted treatment.

Modern living

Basic research continues into links between allergies and food, air, water, homes, pollution, lifestyle, climate change, and almost every other aspect of modern life. Better understanding of allergies may allow parents to reduce the risks of their children developing them, for example, by avoiding certain foods in the first year of life. Supporters of the hygiene hypothesis suggest that exposure to a carefully tested mix of microbes and common allergens early in life may reduce the general risk of developing an allergy later. This could work in the same way as the vaccines or immunizations given as injections against diseases such as polio, measles, mumps, and rubella (German measles).

Genetic research

It may also be possible to use the fast-growing base of genetic information and new technologies to fight allergies. If the precise makeup of common allergens can be determined, this could lead to vaccines against them. Or plants and even animals might be genetically modified so they do not produce allergens, either when alive or when eaten as foods. However, there does not seem to be a magic drug or wonder cure method for allergies in the near future.

Information and Advice

Many organizations offer advice about allergies and have hot lines giving further information.

Contacts

Allergy and Asthma Network Mothers of Asthmatics
2751 Prosperity Avenue, Suite 150
Fairfax, VA 22031
Phone: 800-878-4403
Website: www.breatherville.org
Founded in 1985, Allergy and Asthma Network Mothers of Asthmatics is a national nonprofit network of families whose desire is to overcome, not cope with, allergies and asthma. AANMA's mission is to produce the most accurate, timely, practical, and livable alternatives to suffering.

American Academy of Allergy, Asthma, and Immunology
611 East Wells Street
Milwaukee, WI 53202
Phone: 414-272-6071
Patient information and physician referral hot line: 800-822-2762
Website: www.aaaai.org
The American Academy of Allergy, Asthma, and Immunology is the largest professional medical specialty organization representing allergists, clinical immunologists, allied health professionals, and other physicians with a special interest in allergy. Its mission is the advancement of the knowledge and practice of allergy, asthma, and immunology for optimal patient care.

American College of Allergy, Asthma, and Immunology
85 West Algonquin Road, Suite 550
Arlington Heights, IL 60005
Phone: 847-427-1200
Website: www.allergy.mcg.edu
The American College of Allergy, Asthma, and Immunology is an organization of allergists, immunologists, and related health-care professionals dedicated to quality patient care through research, advocacy, and professional and public education. The Allergy, Asthma, and Immunology Online website is associated with the college.

Asthma and Allergy Foundation of America
1233 20th Street, NW, Suite 402
Washington, DC 20036
Phone: 202-466-7643
Hot line: 800-7-ASTHMA
Website: www.aafa.org
The Asthma and Allergy Foundation of America is a not-for-profit organization dedicated to finding a cure for and controlling asthma and allergic diseases. The organization has a national and thirteen local chapters throughout the United States.

Food Allergy and Anaphylaxis Network
10400 Eaton Place, Suite 107
Fairfax, VA 22030-2208
Phone: 800-929-4040
Website: www.foodallergy.org
The Food Allergy & Anaphylaxis Network (FAAN) was established in 1991 to be a world leader in food allergy and anaphylaxis awareness, and the issues surrounding this condition. The organization also maintains FANTeen, (www.fankids.org/FANTeen), a website designed for young adults who want to take a more active role in managing their food allergies.

More Books to Read

Bryan, Jenny. *Asthma.* Chicago: Heinemann Library, 2004.

Edelson, Edward. *Allergies.* Broomall, Pa.: Chelsea House, 1999.

Giuliucci, Mark. *Allergies: What You Need to Know.* Alexandria, Va., 1999.

Lennard-Brown, Sarah. *Allergies.* Chicago: Raintree, 2004.

Monroe, Judy. Allergies. Minnetonka, Minn.: Capstone Press, 2003.

Moragne, Wendy. *Allergies.* Brooklyn, N.Y.: Millbrook Press, 1999.

Munoz-Furlong, Anne, ed. *Stories from the Heart: A Collection of Essays from Teens with Food Allergies.* Fairfax, Va.: Food Allergy & Anaphylaxis Network, 2000.

Peters, Celeste A. *Allergies, Asthma, and Exercise: The Science of Health.* Chicago: Raintree, 2000.

Schwartz, Robert H., and Peter M. G. Deane. *Coping with Allergies.* New York: Rosen Publishing, 1999.

Glossary

allergen
substance that causes an allergic reaction

allergic reaction
body's response to a normally harmless substance, an allergen, which causes effects such as swelling, redness, itching, and fluid buildup in various areas

anesthetic
substance that lessens or removes feelings and sensations, including touch and pain

anaphylaxis
sudden and severe allergic reaction that may interfere with breathing and cause heart problems, and may threaten life. Anaphylaxis requires emergency medical treatment.

antibiotic
drug that kills bacteria or prevents their growth and that can cure infections

antibody
substance made by the body to kill or damage invading germs or other harmful items

asthma
allergy-based condition that usually causes wheezing and difficulty in breathing

atopic
tendency to develop allergic conditions, in particular those such as eczema, asthma, and hay fever

aversion
dislike of something

dander
tiny particles of skin, fur, feathers, or other substances from animals

decongestant
substance that lessens congestion, or the buildup of fluids and mucus in or on a body part, such as when the nose is stuffed up

dermatitis
skin condition usually caused by an allergy in which patches of skin become red, sore, and itchy or dry, scaly, or moist (often also called eczema)

dust mite
tiny eight-legged creature that lives in house dust and whose feces can cause allergic reactions in some people

eczema
skin condition usually caused by an allergy in which patches of skin become red, sore, and itchy or dry, scaly, or moist (often also called dermatitis)

emollient
substance that softens and soothes the skin

gene
part of chromosomes that carries instructions for how the body develops and carries out life processes

glandular fever
infection causing fever, headache, sore throat, and swollen glands, mainly in the neck, but also in the armpits and groin. It is sometimes accompanied by a rash.

hepatitis B
infection of the liver causing weakness, digestive problems, yellowing of the skin, fever, appetite loss, nausea, and other symptoms

histamine
body chemical that causes symptoms of an allergy, such as swelling, redness, itching, and fluid buildup in the affected parts

hygiene hypothesis
theory about why allergies develop in certain people, based on the idea that the body's surroundings are too clean and the body does not encounter enough germs or other problems

hypoallergenic
containing only very small amounts of possible allergens

immune system
body's own self-defense system, which fights infection and provides resistance to disease

immunotherapy
medical treatment that uses certain parts of the immune system to fight disease

inflammation
condition in which a part of the body becomes red, sore, and swollen because of an infection or injury

intolerance
being unable to deal with or cope with something, either in behavior or in the body's processes

mast cell
microscopic body cell that is part of the immune system and that releases the body chemical histamine during an allergic reaction

microbe
microscopic living thing. Microbes include harmful types of germs such as bacteria and viruses.

mucus
slimy fluid produced by the body, especially by the inner linings of the nose, mouth, throat, airways, lungs, gullet, stomach, and intestines

perennial
occurring or being present more or less all the time, rather than periodically or seasonally

rhinitis
inflammation, redness, soreness, and fluid buildup in the nose and nasal passages, usually in their linings. It causes sneezing, itching, blockage or dripping, and general irritation.

sensitization
period of time after a person has first been exposed to an allergen, during which the immune system learns to recognize the substance

steroid
medication used to prevent or reduce swelling, congestion, redness, and other features of inflammation

toxicity
level at which something is toxic (poisonous or harmful in some way)

trigger
something that can set off a reaction or process

tuberculosis
serious infection that causes fever, weakness, coughing and breathing problems and other symptoms

urticaria
skin condition with pale, flat-topped, red-edged lumps or welts that itch or sting. It can be caused by stinging or poisonous plants or animals or by an allergic reaction.

Index